DIY Smart Home on a Budget

Automate Your House Today

By Techno Cedo

Book content:

Chapter 1: Introduction to Smart Homes

Section 1: What Is a Smart Home?

Section 2: Benefits and Budget Considerations

Chapter 2: Building the Foundation

Section 1: Essential Tools and Platforms

Section 2: Home Network and Power Setup

Chapter 3: Lighting Automation

Section 1: Smart Bulbs and Switches

Section 2: Light Scenes and Automation

Chapter 4: Smart Security Systems

Section 1: Cameras, Alarms, and Entry Sensors

Section 2: Remote Monitoring and Alerts

Chapter 5: Climate Control and Energy Efficiency

Section 1: Smart Thermostats and Fans

Section 2: Monitoring and Reducing Energy Use

Chapter 6: Entertainment and Lifestyle Automation

Section 1: Media Centers and Smart Speakers

Section 2: DIY Projects for Daily Convenience

Chapter 7: Maintenance, Safety & Expansion

Section 1: Keeping Your Smart Home Secure

Section 2: Planning for Growth

Chapter 1: Introduction to Smart Homes

Section 1: What Is a Smart Home?

The Evolution of Home Automation

The idea of a home that can think, respond, and anticipate our needs has long fascinated inventors, scientists, and homeowners alike. From the pages of science fiction to the reality of modern-day living, the smart home has evolved from a futuristic concept to a practical, accessible solution for everyday life.

The earliest seeds of home automation can be traced back to the late 19th and early 20th centuries with the invention of labor-saving household appliances. The arrival of electricity into homes enabled the development of electric washing machines, refrigerators, and vacuum cleaners; technologies that revolutionized domestic life. Though not "smart" in today's sense, these inventions marked the beginning of homes designed for efficiency and convenience.

The concept of true automation emerged in the 1960s and 1970s. The **ECHO IV**, developed in 1966, is often considered the first real attempt at a smart home computer. It could compute shopping lists, control the home's temperature, and turn appliances on and off. However, it was not commercially viable due to its complexity and cost.

In the 1980s and 1990s, home automation was primarily the domain of the wealthy or technologically inclined. Systems were often custom-built and relied on complex wiring. X10, a communication protocol developed in 1975, allowed compatible devices to communicate over a home's electrical wiring. While it offered remote control over lights and appliances, it was unreliable and prone to signal interference.

The major turning point came with the rise of the internet and wireless technology. The 2000s saw the introduction of Wi-Fi-enabled devices and smartphones, which enabled real-time control over home systems. Devices could now be monitored and adjusted remotely, opening the door to broader adoption.

By the 2010s, major technology players like **Google, Amazon, and Apple** began entering the market with smart speakers, thermostats, and hubs. Products like the **Nest Thermostat** (acquired by Google in 2014) and **Amazon Echo** (released in 2015) made it easier than ever for the average consumer to begin automating their homes without any technical background.

Today, smart home technology has become affordable, modular, and user-friendly. Consumers can start small (with a single smart plug or bulb) and gradually build up their systems. The rise of **DIY-friendly platforms** and open-source tools like **Home Assistant** has further accelerated adoption. The future of smart homes is now focused on interconnectivity, **energy efficiency**, **security**, and **affordability**; making it the perfect time to begin your own DIY smart home journey.

Components of a Smart Home

Understanding what makes a home "smart" begins with recognizing its core components. While each smart home is unique and can be customized to individual needs, most systems share a set of fundamental building blocks. Here's a breakdown of the essential components that make up a modern DIY smart home:

1. Smart Hubs and Controllers

A smart hub is the **brain** of a smart home system. It connects and coordinates communication between various devices, even if they come from different brands or use different communication protocols (like Wi-Fi, Zigbee, or Z-Wave). While not every system requires a hub (many Wi-Fi-based devices can function independently) hubs become important as you scale up.

Popular examples include:

- **Amazon Echo (Alexa)**: Doubles as a smart speaker and voice assistant. Compatible with a wide range of devices.
- **Google Nest Hub**: Offers voice control and visual feedback through a touchscreen.
- **Apple HomePod**: Works with Apple's HomeKit ecosystem for privacy-focused automation.
- **SmartThings Hub**: A powerful hub that connects Zigbee and Z-Wave devices for advanced control.
- **Home Assistant**: A free, open-source platform that runs on devices like the Raspberry Pi. It allows complete customization and local control, appealing to DIY users.

Each hub has strengths and weaknesses. Some are easier to set up, while others offer deeper customization. Choosing the right hub depends on your needs, budget, and level of technical skill.

2. Voice Assistants

Voice assistants like **Amazon Alexa**, **Google Assistant**, and **Apple Siri** have made controlling smart devices effortless. They act as both an interface and a controller. Using simple voice commands, you can turn off lights, adjust the thermostat, lock doors, or play music.

These assistants are integrated into smart speakers and displays, making them central to modern smart homes. They also support routines; predefined sets of actions triggered by a single command like "Good Morning" or "Movie Time."

For example:

- "Alexa, good morning" might turn on your lights, read the weather, and start the coffee maker.
- "Hey Google, I'm home" could unlock the door, adjust the thermostat, and play music.

Voice control is particularly useful for those with limited mobility or for moments when your hands are full.

3. Sensors and Triggers

Sensors play a crucial role in making a home *intelligent*, not just automated. Rather than relying solely on manual input, sensors allow devices to react to real-world conditions.

Common types of smart sensors include:

- **Motion Sensors**: Detect movement to turn on lights or trigger alarms.
- **Contact Sensors**: Installed on doors and windows to monitor entry and exit.
- **Temperature and Humidity Sensors**: Help regulate climate control and ventilation.
- **Water Leak Sensors**: Alert you to leaks near sinks, washing machines, or hot water tanks.
- **Smoke and Carbon Monoxide Detectors**: Send notifications and trigger safety routines.

These sensors can often be connected to your hub to create **automated routines**. For example, a motion sensor can trigger a light when someone walks into a room or alert you if someone enters your home unexpectedly.

4. Smart Plugs and Outlets

Smart plugs are one of the most affordable and versatile devices in a DIY setup. They allow you to turn traditional devices (like lamps, coffee makers, or fans) into smart devices. Simply plug them in and control them via an app or voice command.

Advanced smart plugs also include **energy monitoring features**, enabling you to track power usage and identify which appliances are costing you the most.

5. Smart Lighting

Smart lighting includes bulbs, switches, and dimmers that can be controlled remotely. Most smart bulbs allow for color changes, dimming, and scene control. You can program lighting to match your daily routine, enhance security by mimicking occupancy, or even sync with music and movies.

Affordable options like **TP-Link Kasa**, **Wyze**, and **Philips Wiz** offer easy integration without a hub, while more advanced systems like **Philips Hue** provide a premium experience with a dedicated bridge.

6. Climate Control Devices

Smart thermostats, such as the **Nest Thermostat** or **Ecobee**, help regulate home temperatures while learning your schedule and preferences. They can save energy by automatically adjusting when you're away or asleep.

Other devices like **smart air conditioners**, **fans**, and **humidifiers** can be controlled via smart plugs or built-in Wi-Fi features, allowing you to maintain comfort without wasting energy.

7. Smart Security Devices

Security is a major driver for smart home adoption. Core components include:

- **Smart Cameras**: Indoor and outdoor models that offer real-time video and motion alerts.
- **Video Doorbells**: Allow you to see and speak with visitors via your smartphone.
- **Smart Locks**: Enable keyless entry, remote locking/unlocking, and access sharing.
- **Alarm Systems**: DIY kits often include motion sensors, door sensors, and a central siren.

These systems can notify you instantly if something seems wrong, and many are designed for easy installation and no monthly fees.

8. Apps and Automations

Each smart home ecosystem comes with a companion app that serves as a control center. Through these apps, you can:

- Set schedules and routines
- Monitor devices remotely
- Create automations using "if-this-then-that" logic (e.g., If the sun sets, then turn on porch light)
- Get notifications and alerts

Popular apps include **Amazon Alexa**, **Google Home**, **Apple Home**, **SmartThings**, and **Home Assistant**.

The smart home has transformed from a niche luxury into an accessible and empowering DIY project for anyone with a modest budget and a bit of curiosity. With just a few affordable components (like a smart plug, a voice assistant, and a motion sensor) you can begin automating daily tasks, improving security, and enhancing comfort.

This chapter explored how smart homes evolved from futuristic dreams to practical reality and introduced you to the essential building blocks of a smart home. In the next section, we'll explore how to begin planning your own system, keeping your **budget** and **goals** in mind.

Section 2: Benefits and Budget Considerations

Why Automate?

Smart homes have become more than just a technological trend; they're a practical, everyday solution for simplifying modern life. But why should you consider automating your home, especially if you're on a budget? In this section, we'll explore the top reasons people invest in smart home systems and how those benefits can significantly impact your life, even with minimal upfront investment.

Energy Savings

One of the most immediate and measurable benefits of a smart home is energy efficiency. With energy prices fluctuating and environmental awareness on the rise, many homeowners are looking for ways to cut down on electricity and gas consumption. Smart home technology offers numerous ways to achieve that.

For instance, a **smart thermostat** learns your habits and adjusts the temperature based on whether you're home, asleep, or away. According to **Nest's internal studies**, users saved up to 15% on cooling and 10–12% on heating bills annually.

Similarly, **smart lighting systems** can turn off automatically when no one is in the room or dim during daylight hours. Motion sensors can detect presence, and smart plugs can cut power to unused appliances, reducing "phantom load" energy consumption.

These small adjustments (automated and optimized) add up quickly. Over the course of a year, a budget-friendly setup using just a smart thermostat, plugs, and LED bulbs could save you **hundreds of dollars** in utility bills, paying for itself and then some.

Convenience and Comfort

Convenience is often the number one reason people turn to home automation. Imagine walking into your house after a long day and having your lights turn on automatically, your favorite playlist start playing, and your thermostat adjust to the perfect temperature; all without lifting a finger.

Smart homes allow you to:

- Control everything from your phone or tablet
- Schedule tasks to happen automatically
- Use voice commands to manage devices hands-free
- Set up "scenes" that bundle multiple actions together (e.g., "movie night" might dim lights, close curtains, and turn on the TV)

This level of control not only saves time but enhances your overall comfort and quality of life. For busy families, people with disabilities, or anyone who values simplicity, smart home automation offers an unmatched layer of convenience.

Security and Peace of Mind

Security is another powerful motivator for smart home adoption. With crime and property theft always a concern, many people feel safer knowing their home is monitored; whether they're inside it or miles away.

Smart home security features can include:

- **Door and window sensors** that alert you when someone enters
- **Video doorbells** that let you see and talk to visitors remotely
- **Smart locks** that allow you to grant (and revoke) access from your phone
- **Motion-activated cameras** that send real-time alerts to your device
- **Automated lights** that mimic your presence when you're away

What's more, these features often don't require expensive professional installation. Many DIY security kits are affordable, wireless, and scalable, making them perfect for renters, first-time users, or budget-conscious homeowners.

Even basic systems provide peace of mind; like getting a notification that your front door was left open, or watching a package delivery live while you're at work. Security doesn't have to be complicated or costly, and with the right tools, it can be seamlessly integrated into daily life.

How to Plan a Budget-Friendly System

Creating a smart home doesn't require a massive investment or technical expertise. With a well-thought-out plan and a realistic budget, you can automate key aspects of your home without overspending. In this section, we'll walk through the steps of designing a DIY smart home system that works for you and your wallet.

Set Clear Goals

The first step in building a smart home on a budget is understanding **why** you're doing it. What specific problems are you trying to solve? Avoid falling into the trap of buying flashy gadgets just because they're popular.

Ask yourself:

- Do I want to save energy?
- Do I need to improve home security?
- Do I want more control over my lighting or climate?
- Am I looking to simplify daily routines?

Write down your goals and rank them in order of importance. This clarity will guide every purchasing decision and help you avoid unnecessary spending on devices you won't use or need.

Start Small and Scale Over Time

You don't need to automate your entire home all at once. In fact, it's smarter and more budget-conscious to start small and expand over time. Begin with a few key devices that address your top goals.

Here's a sample path:

- **Step 1:** Buy a smart plug or bulb to get used to automation.
- **Step 2:** Add a voice assistant like Amazon Echo Dot or Google Nest Mini.
- **Step 3:** Install a smart thermostat or smart lock if your budget allows.
- **Step 4:** Gradually introduce motion sensors, cameras, or smart switches.

This gradual approach spreads out your investment and lets you learn along the way. You can also evaluate what's working and what's not, refining your setup based on real experience.

Do Your Research and Compare Options

Not all smart devices are created equal. Prices can vary widely, and more expensive doesn't always mean better. Before buying, take time to:

- **Read reviews** from real users
- **Compare features** across different brands
- **Check compatibility** with your chosen ecosystem (Amazon Alexa, Google Assistant, Apple HomeKit, etc.)
- Look for deals, bundles, or open-box items
- Consider refurbished products from certified retailers

Websites like **Wirecutter, CNET,** and **SmartHomeSolver** offer regular product comparisons and budget-friendly recommendations.

Avoid Unnecessary Subscriptions

Some devices come with optional subscription services for cloud storage, advanced features, or 24/7 monitoring. While these services can be useful, they're not always necessar; especially when you're on a tight budget.

Look for:

- **Cameras with local storage**
- **Free-tier apps with basic automation capabilities**
- **Home hubs like Home Assistant that offer local control and no monthly fees**

By skipping subscriptions, you retain more control and reduce long-term costs.

Stick to Interoperable Platforms

Nothing drives up costs like needing multiple apps, hubs, or proprietary accessories to make your devices work. Focus on building your system around a platform that supports **wide compatibility**.

Amazon Alexa and Google Assistant are good choices for beginners, while Home Assistant and SmartThings offer deeper integration for tech-savvy users. Also consider choosing products that support common communication protocols like:

- **Wi-Fi**: Easy to set up but can strain your router
- **Zigbee/Z-Wave**: Reliable mesh networks for advanced setups
- **Matter**: A new universal standard backed by Google, Apple, Amazon, and more

Choosing interoperable devices avoids the frustration and expense of incompatible gear and streamlines your smart home journey.

DIY Installation Over Professional Services

Many smart home products are designed with DIY users in mind. They come with simple instructions, adhesive mounts, or easy screw-in fixtures. Opting for self-installation not only saves money but helps you better understand how your system works.

For instance:

- Smart plugs just plug into your existing outlets
- Most smart bulbs screw into standard light sockets
- Door and window sensors come with peel-and-stick adhesive
- Smart thermostats include clear wiring diagrams and setup videos

If you're ever unsure, online communities like **Reddit's r/smarthome** or **YouTube tutorials** can be incredibly helpful. With a little patience and curiosity, you can install most devices in under 30 minutes.

A smart home offers a combination of energy savings, convenience, and peace of mind; all of which are within reach, even on a modest budget. Whether you want to reduce your utility bills, simplify daily routines, or keep your home secure, smart technology can help you achieve your goals.

The key to success is in **careful planning**, **prioritizing your needs**, and **starting small**. Avoid the temptation to buy unnecessary gadgets, and instead focus on building a system that solves real problems in your life.

As we move forward in this book, you'll learn step-by-step how to choose, install, and automate devices for every room in your home. With the right approach, you'll create a customized smart home that works for your budget, your lifestyle, and your future.

Chapter 2: Building the Foundation

Section 1: Essential Tools and Platforms

When building your smart home, the foundation you set is critical to how smoothly everything functions in the future. One of the first decisions you'll make is choosing a smart hub, which acts as the brain of your smart home. Along with that, you'll need a basic set of tools and software to carry out installations and troubleshoot issues. This chapter will walk you through the essential platforms and tools, with a focus on keeping costs low and efficiency high.

Choosing a Smart Hub

A **smart hub** is a central device or software that connects all your smart home gadgets. It coordinates communication between lights, thermostats, cameras, sensors, and voice assistants. Think of it as the conductor of your home's automation orchestra. The three most popular hubs for DIY smart homes are Amazon Alexa, Google Assistant, and Home Assistant. Each platform comes with its own strengths, limitations, and ecosystem compatibility.

1. Amazon Alexa

Pros:

- **Wide Device Compatibility**: Alexa is compatible with thousands of smart home devices including lights, cameras, switches, plugs, and even refrigerators. It integrates well with brands like TP-Link, Philips Hue, Ring, and Ecobee.
- **User-Friendly Setup**: The Alexa app makes device setup and grouping very intuitive, even for beginners. You can set routines (e.g., "Good Morning" turns on lights and starts the coffee maker) with just a few taps.
- **Routine Automation**: Alexa allows you to create routines triggered by voice, schedules, or sensors, enhancing automation without any coding.

Cons:

- **Cloud Reliant**: Most of Alexa's features rely on cloud connectivity. If your internet goes down, many automations stop working.
- **Limited Local Control**: Unlike Home Assistant, Alexa doesn't offer much in terms of local device control. This affects speed and privacy.
- **Privacy Concerns**: Always-listening microphones and cloud storage of voice commands have raised privacy red flags among users.

2. Google Assistant (Google Home)

Pros:

- **Advanced Natural Language Processing**: Google Assistant is extremely good at understanding natural language and contextual queries. You can ask, "What's the weather like at my mom's house?" and it knows what you mean.
- **Integration with Google Services**: Seamlessly connects to Gmail, Calendar, Google Maps, and YouTube, which adds layers of functionality. For example, your morning routine can include commute updates from Google Maps.
- **Growing Device Ecosystem**: Google has rapidly expanded compatibility, supporting Nest, Philips Hue, Wyze, and more.

Cons:

- **Still Cloud-Based**: Like Alexa, Google Assistant requires internet access for most operations.
- **Less Custom Automation**: It offers fewer automation customization options compared to Alexa and significantly less than Home Assistant.
- **Occasional App Complexity**: The Google Home app can be less intuitive, particularly when setting up new devices or organizing them into rooms.

3. Home Assistant

Pros:

- **Local Control**: One of the biggest benefits of Home Assistant is that it runs locally, so you aren't reliant on the internet or cloud servers. This improves privacy, speed, and reliability.
- **Deep Customization**: Allows for complex automations using YAML, Node-RED, or visual editors. You can create advanced automations like "If it's cloudy and the indoor light level is below X, turn on the living room lights."
- **Open-Source**: There's a massive community contributing integrations, plugins, and support. It supports over 1,800 integrations natively.

Cons:

- **Learning Curve**: Home Assistant can be intimidating for beginners. YAML configuration files and system updates require a bit of tech-savviness.
- **Manual Setup**: Many integrations require manual configuration, which can be time-consuming.
- **Hardware Requirement**: Requires dedicated hardware like a Raspberry Pi, mini PC, or virtual machine to run reliably.

Basic Tools You'll Need

Once your smart hub is chosen, the next step is to gather essential tools to install and manage your devices. These tools don't have to be expensive. Many can be found in your local hardware store or even your garage. Below is a breakdown of essential categories and recommended items.

1. Hand Tools for Installation

These basic tools help you physically install most smart devices, such as door sensors, thermostats, or smart light switches.

Screwdrivers

- A good **Phillips-head** and **flat-head screwdriver** set is vital. Many smart gadgets need light disassembly for battery insertion or wall mounting.
- Opt for a magnetic set for ease of use when handling tiny screws.

Wire Strippers

- Especially useful when installing smart light switches or thermostats. Wire strippers allow clean and safe stripping of insulation from wires.

Pliers and Wire Cutters

- **Needle-nose pliers** help position small wires, while **wire cutters** are necessary for trimming wires during installation.

Power Drill

- A basic cordless power drill makes mounting devices on drywall or masonry much easier.
- Consider getting a drill bit set that includes anchors and screws compatible with different surfaces.

2. Electrical and Safety Testing Tools

Smart homes often involve some light electrical work. Even replacing a light switch or installing a smart plug can involve exposure to wiring.

Voltage Tester

- A non-contact **voltage tester** ensures you're not working on a live circuit. This is essential for safety.
- They're inexpensive (under $15) and easy to use.

Multimeter

- Measures voltage, current, and resistance. Useful for diagnosing wiring issues when devices aren't powering on.
- Even a basic digital multimeter can significantly help with troubleshooting.

Cable Testers

- If you're wiring Ethernet cables or troubleshooting smart cameras, a **network cable tester** helps ensure the integrity of your connections.

3. Digital Tools and Apps

Your smartphone or tablet becomes your main interface to your smart home. Several apps and software tools will help you manage your ecosystem smoothly.

Manufacturer Apps

- **Alexa app** (iOS/Android)
- **Google Home app**
- **Home Assistant Companion app**

These apps help you add devices, group them by room, create routines, and monitor activity.

Network Scanner

- Tools like **Fing** (free on Android and iOS) show all devices on your home network, their IP addresses, and connection status. Excellent for diagnosing connectivity problems.

Automation Platforms

- **IFTTT (If This Then That)** is useful if you're trying to connect services or devices that don't natively support each other.
- **Tasker** (Android only) allows more custom automations on your phone.

Voice Assistant Apps

- If you're using Alexa or Google, having the **voice assistant apps** installed on all family phones increases convenience and expands control across the household.

4. Optional But Helpful Tools

Label Maker or Tape and Marker

- When wiring multiple devices, labeling wires can prevent future confusion.

Smartphone Mount or Tripod

- Great for watching video tutorials while installing a device hands-free.

QR Code Scanner App

- Many smart devices use QR codes for pairing. A scanner app can speed up setup, though your camera app may suffice.

Building a DIY smart home on a budget starts with a solid foundation. Selecting the right smart hub is not just about brand preference; it's about what works for your home, your skill level, and your privacy expectations. Whether you prefer the simplicity of Alexa or Google Assistant, or the deep customization of Home Assistant, each has a role in building an efficient, automated home.

Equally important are the tools that enable installation, testing, and maintenance. The good news is you don't need to break the bank to get started. Many of the tools mentioned in this chapter are affordable and widely available. In fact, with a budget of under $100, you could equip yourself with everything needed to install most DIY smart devices.

Armed with a smart hub and a toolbox, you're now ready to move forward with planning and installing your system. In the next section, we'll dive into network setup and configuration; the true backbone of any smart home.

Section 2: Home Network and Power Setup

In any smart home, the invisible forces of connectivity and power are just as important as the smart devices themselves. Without a strong, stable Wi-Fi connection or safe power delivery, your gadgets will struggle to perform at their best. Whether you're setting up smart lights, cameras, thermostats, or speakers, ensuring that your home network and power infrastructure can support them is a critical step. This section dives deep into how to optimize your Wi-Fi for smart devices and how to manage power usage safely and efficiently using smart plugs and surge protectors.

Wi-Fi Optimization for Smart Devices

Understanding the Role of Wi-Fi

Smart devices rely heavily on your home's Wi-Fi network to communicate with one another and with cloud servers. If your Wi-Fi is weak, slow, or inconsistent, devices may become unresponsive, experience delays, or fail to function entirely. The more smart devices you add, the more strain you place on your network. That's why optimizing your Wi-Fi setup is foundational.

Choosing the Right Router

Not all routers are created equal. When building a smart home, it is highly recommended to invest in a dual-band or tri-band router that supports both 2.4GHz and 5GHz frequencies.

- **2.4GHz band** is slower but offers a longer range. Most smart devices prefer this band.
- **5GHz band** is faster but has a shorter range.
- **Tri-band routers** add an extra 5GHz band to balance high data usage among devices.

Look for routers that support Wi-Fi 5 (802.11ac) or Wi-Fi 6 (802.11ax). Wi-Fi 6 offers improved performance, especially for crowded networks.

Router Placement

The physical location of your router has a big impact on Wi-Fi performance. Ideally, place your router:

- In a central location
- Away from metal objects and appliances like microwaves
- Elevated (e.g., on a shelf or wall)

Avoid placing your router in a cabinet or behind large furniture, as these can obstruct the signal.

Mesh Networks

For larger homes or homes with multiple floors, a mesh Wi-Fi system can ensure consistent coverage throughout. Mesh systems consist of a main router and satellite nodes that communicate with each other, creating a blanket of coverage.

Popular mesh systems include Google Nest Wi-Fi, Eero, and Netgear Orbi. These are especially useful if you plan to place smart devices in areas far from your main router, such as a garage or backyard.

Device Prioritization and Network Segmentation

Some routers allow you to prioritize certain devices or set up separate networks:

- **Device Prioritization:** Ensures critical devices (like smart cameras or thermostats) always have enough bandwidth.
- **Guest Network:** Separate your smart home devices from your main devices (phones, laptops) to improve security and reduce congestion.

Signal Boosting and Extenders

If mesh networks are too expensive, Wi-Fi extenders or repeaters can be used to amplify the signal. These devices are more affordable but may reduce overall speed.

Safe Power Management and Smart Plugs

Why Power Management Matters

Smart homes include many devices that consume electricity and need to be powered safely. Faulty wiring, overloads, or surges can damage devices and pose fire risks. Implementing a sound power management strategy ensures your smart home is not only functional but safe.

Surge Protectors

Surge protectors are essential when dealing with sensitive electronics. A power surge, often caused by lightning or grid switching, can damage or destroy devices.

When selecting a surge protector:

- **Joule Rating**: Choose a protector with a high joule rating (1000 joules or higher).
- **Clamping Voltage**: Lower clamping voltage is better (look for 330V).
- **UL Certification**: Ensures safety standards are met.

Some surge protectors come with USB ports or network protection features, which can be handy for smart hubs and routers.

Smart Plugs: The Power of Control

Smart plugs offer more than just on/off capabilities. They add automation and monitoring to regular outlets, allowing you to control connected devices via smartphone apps or voice commands.

Features to Look For:

- **Remote Control:** Turn devices on/off from anywhere.
- **Scheduling:** Automate when devices turn on or off.
- **Energy Monitoring:** Track power usage to identify energy hogs.
- **Integration:** Ensure compatibility with Alexa, Google Assistant, or Home Assistant.

Popular smart plug brands include TP-Link Kasa, Wemo, and Amazon Smart Plug.

Common Uses:

- Automating coffee makers or lamps
- Turning off idle electronics to save energy
- Scheduling space heaters or fans
- Simulating presence when away from home

Power Strip with Smart Outlets

Advanced power strips offer multiple individually-controlled smart outlets. These are excellent for entertainment centers or workstations with multiple connected devices.

Some also include surge protection, making them a 2-in-1 solution.

Avoiding Overloads

Smart devices often consume low power, but combining several into one outlet can still create risks.

- Avoid plugging too many devices into one power strip.
- Check the wattage ratings of your plugs and strips.
- Do not daisy-chain multiple power strips.

Battery Backup (UPS)

Uninterruptible Power Supplies (UPS) can keep critical devices like routers, smart hubs, or cameras running during short power outages. This can prevent automation disruptions and maintain security.

Look for UPS units with:

- Sufficient wattage and runtime
- LCD displays for monitoring
- USB and Ethernet surge protection

Putting It All Together

Setting up your home's network and power structure is not a one-size-fits-all task. However, following these basic principles will help:

Example Setup for a Small Home

- **Router**: Dual-band Wi-Fi 6 router placed centrally
- **Smart Plug**: One per major room
- **Surge Protector**: One per major appliance or entertainment center
- **UPS**: For modem, router, and Home Assistant hub

Example Setup for a Large Home

- **Mesh Network**: Three-node system covering all floors
- **Smart Power Strips**: For rooms with multiple gadgets
- **Voltage Tester**: For safe DIY installation
- **Dedicated Guest Network**: For smart devices

Tips for Long-Term Maintenance

1. **Regularly Update Firmware:** Keep your router and smart plugs up-to-date to patch security vulnerabilities.
2. **Monitor Device Count:** As you add more devices, periodically check network performance.

3. **Label Everything:** Label your smart plugs and surge protectors for easier troubleshooting.
4. **Keep a Backup Plan:** Have manual overrides in place (manual switches, remote access apps).

Building a smart home is about more than just flashy gadgets. A solid Wi-Fi setup and safe power management system are crucial to making sure those gadgets perform reliably and safely. Optimizing your network ensures that devices stay connected and responsive, while using smart plugs and surge protectors gives you the control and safety you need.

As we move forward in building your smart home, these foundational components will support every automation and smart device you install. With the basics in place, you're now ready to explore device installation and automation setup in the chapters to come.

Section 1: Smart Bulbs and Switches

Installing Smart Bulbs on a Budget

Smart lighting is often the first step many homeowners take when starting their journey into home automation. It's accessible, cost-effective, and delivers immediate benefits in convenience, energy savings, and ambiance control. For those working with a limited budget, knowing how to pick and install the right smart bulbs can make all the difference.

Choosing Cost-Effective Smart Bulbs

The market is filled with smart lighting options, from well-known brands like Philips Hue and LIFX to more budget-friendly alternatives such as Wyze, Sengled, and Kasa by TP-Link. While premium brands offer advanced features and broader compatibility, many affordable models deliver excellent performance at a fraction of the cost.

When evaluating smart bulbs on a budget, consider the following key features:

- **Wi-Fi vs. Hub-Dependent:** Bulbs that connect directly to Wi-Fi, like those from Wyze or Kasa, are ideal for budget-conscious users. They eliminate the need for an additional hub, simplifying setup and reducing cost.
- **Dimming and Color Options:** Many affordable bulbs still offer dimming capabilities and a range of white temperatures or even full-color options. These features help customize the atmosphere of your rooms without breaking the bank.
- **App and Voice Assistant Integration:** Ensure the bulb works with your existing ecosystem (Amazon Alexa, Google Assistant, or Apple HomeKit) so you can control lighting via voice or mobile app.

A 4-pack of white smart bulbs from Wyze or Sengled, for instance, can often be found for under $30. This offers a low-risk entry point to test automation benefits in a couple of rooms before expanding.

Setting Up and Scheduling Smart Bulbs

Installation is usually as simple as screwing in the bulb and pairing it with the appropriate mobile app. Once the bulb is connected, you can create lighting schedules, routines, or automations. For example:

- **Morning Wake-Up:** Set the bulb to gradually brighten in the morning to mimic sunrise and promote natural waking.
- **Away Mode:** Automatically turn lights on and off while you're away to simulate occupancy.
- **Movie Time Scene:** Set dim lighting with a single voice command or tap in the app.

These schedules reduce manual control, increase energy efficiency, and add a layer of security by making your home appear occupied even when it's not.

Converting Traditional Switches

While smart bulbs are excellent, they're not always the best solution; especially in households where light switches are still commonly used. Turning off a smart bulb at the switch cuts power entirely, rendering app and voice control useless. That's where smart switches come into play.

Affordable Smart Switch Options

Smart switches replace your traditional wall switches and maintain power to smart bulbs or control standard bulbs themselves. They work independently of the bulb and integrate seamlessly with most smart home ecosystems. Affordable brands include:

- **Kasa Smart Light Switch by TP-Link:** Often available for under $20, it supports both single-pole installations and works with Alexa and Google Assistant.
- **Treatlife Smart Switches:** Known for affordability and compatibility with both Google and Alexa, these switches offer scheduling and scene control.
- **Geeni TAP Smart Switch:** Another cost-effective option with a simple installation process.

Before purchasing, ensure that:

1. You have a neutral wire in your switch box (many smart switches require this).
2. The switch supports your wiring configuration (single-pole vs. 3-way).

Installation Tips for DIYers

Replacing a standard switch with a smart one is relatively straightforward, but basic electrical knowledge and safety precautions are essential:

1. **Turn Off the Circuit:** Always switch off power to the circuit at your main breaker before working.
2. **Label Your Wires:** Use painter's tape or labels to mark existing wire positions before disconnecting anything.
3. **Use the Instructions:** Follow the included installation guide closely. Manufacturers usually provide illustrated manuals and online videos.
4. **Check with a Voltage Tester:** Confirm that the circuit is truly de-energized before touching any wires.

If you're unsure about electrical work, consider hiring an electrician for installation; especially when dealing with complex or older home wiring systems.

Combining Smart Bulbs and Switches

It's worth noting that in some situations, combining smart bulbs with smart switches can cause compatibility issues. For instance, dimmer smart switches may conflict with smart bulbs' internal dimming controls, leading to flickering or limited performance.

To avoid issues:

- Use smart switches with standard (non-smart) LED or incandescent bulbs.
- Use smart bulbs with traditional switches left always "on."
- Consider multi-bulb fixtures where one smart switch can manage multiple traditional bulbs more economically than replacing each bulb with a smart one.

Creating Lighting Zones and Scenes

As your smart lighting setup expands, consider organizing devices into zones; like "Living Room," "Bedroom," or "Porch." This enables whole-room control via a single voice command or app button. Scenes, such as "Relax," "Dinner," or "Work Mode," can adjust brightness and color in multiple bulbs or switches simultaneously.

Apps like Google Home, Amazon Alexa, or Apple Home allow you to create these zones and routines intuitively. For more customization, consider third-party platforms like IFTTT or SmartThings, which provide more advanced automation triggers and multi-device coordination.

Real-Life Budget Example: Two-Room Setup for Under $60

Let's say you want to automate lighting in your living room and bedroom. Here's a sample budget:

- **4 Wyze White Smart Bulbs:** $28
- **2 Kasa Smart Switches:** $35

With this simple setup, you can:

- Schedule your bedroom light to turn on at 6:30 AM and off at 11:00 PM
- Control your living room lighting via voice while watching TV
- Set your front room lights to turn on when your smartphone detects you've arrived home

This basic setup keeps your total cost under $65, leverages voice assistants you may already own, and provides immediate improvements to comfort, security, and energy use.

Lighting automation is one of the most gratifying parts of a smart home, and it's especially accessible to those on a budget. Whether you opt for smart bulbs, smart switches, or a mix of both, you'll find the initial investment modest and the return in convenience and efficiency high. In the next section, we'll explore motion sensors and automation routines that can further enhance your lighting system and bring it to the next level of intelligence and personalization.

Section 2: Light Scenes and Automation

Smart lighting is one of the most accessible and visually impactful ways to transform your home into a smart home. Beyond the novelty of changing bulb colors, modern lighting systems allow you to define "light scenes" that can dramatically alter the mood of a space based on your schedule, activity, or preferences. Coupled with motion sensors, these lighting setups become dynamic and responsive; offering convenience, saving energy, and elevating your day-to-day life.

In this section, we'll dive into two key strategies: creating light scenes for ambiance and integrating motion sensors to automate lighting behavior.

Creating Light Scenes for Ambiance

What Is a Light Scene?

A light scene is a predefined combination of brightness, color temperature, and hue settings across one or more lights that creates a desired mood or setting. Think of them as "presets" for your lighting.

Instead of manually dimming your lights or adjusting individual bulbs, a scene can do it all with one voice command, app tap, or automation trigger. This is especially valuable for multitasking households or those who enjoy ambient experiences tailored to time of day or activity.

Setting Moods for Different Times of Day

Lighting is closely tied to our biological rhythms. By aligning your lighting to your natural schedule, you can promote alertness during the day and relaxation at night. Here are several practical examples of mood-based scenes:

1. Morning Wake-Up Scene
Set your bedroom lights to mimic the rising sun. Start with a warm amber tone at a low brightness around 6:30 AM, and slowly increase to a daylight-white by 7:00 AM. This gentle transition can help regulate circadian rhythms and replace jarring alarms.

2. Focus Mode or Work Scene
In your home office or study area, use cool white light (5000K–6500K) at higher brightness to boost concentration and reduce eye strain. Assign this to weekdays from 9:00 AM to 5:00 PM, and trigger it through a smart assistant or app.

3. Relaxation Scene
After 8:00 PM, switch to soft, warm white lighting (2700K) across your living room and

bedroom. Low brightness and amber tones can help signal to your brain that it's time to wind down.

4. Movie Night Scene

A common favorite, this scene dims all main lights to about 10% and bathes the room in a subtle blue or purple hue. Lights behind the TV can reduce eye fatigue and create an immersive viewing experience.

5. Dinner Party Scene

For social events, combine ambient dimmed ceiling lights with accent lighting from lamps or LED strips. Slightly warmer temperatures around 3000K set a cozy yet elegant tone.

Setting Up Scenes with Your Smart System

Nearly all smart lighting ecosystems (like Philips Hue, LIFX, Govee, or even Alexa-compatible bulbs) offer apps where you can create and manage scenes.

How to Set Up a Scene (Example with Philips Hue):

1. Open the Hue app.
2. Select a room or zone.
3. Tap "New Scene" and choose your lights.
4. Adjust each light's color and brightness.
5. Name your scene and save it.
6. Optionally, schedule it or assign it to a voice command.

Voice Examples:

- "Alexa, activate Morning Scene."
- "Hey Google, set Movie Night."
- "Siri, turn on Relax Lights."

Motion Sensor Integration

Why Use Motion Sensors?

Motion sensors take lighting automation one step further by making your home responsive. Rather than relying on voice commands or timers, your lights can respond to your movements in real time.

They're perfect for utility areas like hallways, closets, bathrooms, garages, and stairwells; spaces where lights are often needed briefly or when your hands are full.

How Motion Sensors Work

A smart motion sensor detects movement within a given range (usually up to 30 feet). Once motion is detected, the sensor sends a signal to your smart hub or lighting system to activate a light scene. Most also include an ambient light sensor, so they'll only trigger lights if it's dark enough.

You can define:

- **Active Time** (e.g., 6 PM to 6 AM)
- **Duration** (e.g., lights stay on for 2 minutes after motion)
- **Brightness Level**
- **Which scene is triggered**

Where to Use Motion Sensors

Here are key areas where motion sensors are most useful:

1. Hallways and Staircases
Avoid fumbling in the dark at night. Install motion sensors near stair entry points to automatically light your path.

2. Bathrooms
Hands-free lighting is particularly useful at night. Configure your lights to activate dimly so as not to shock your eyes during a late-night trip.

3. Kitchens and Pantries
Cooking or carrying groceries often leaves your hands full. A ceiling-mounted motion sensor can automatically light your prep area.

4. Closets
Small spaces like closets often benefit from short-duration lighting that turns on only when accessed.

Popular Motion Sensors for Smart Homes

- **Philips Hue Motion Sensor**
  Integrates seamlessly with Hue bulbs, supports light and motion detection, and allows full customization in the app.

- **Aqara Motion Sensor (Zigbee)**
  Works with Home Assistant and Apple HomeKit. Affordable and battery-efficient.

- **SwitchBot Motion Sensor**
  Easy to use, wide detection angle, and supports Alexa/Google Assistant

integrations.

- **TP-Link Kasa Smart Motion Sensor**
  Budget-friendly and works well with Kasa lighting products.

Combining Motion Sensors with Scenes

Here's how you can make the most of sensors and scenes together:

Scenario 1: Night Bathroom Scene

- Between 10 PM and 6 AM
- Trigger a dim (15%) warm light when motion is detected
- Turn off after 3 minutes of no motion

Scenario 2: Hallway Day/Night Dual Behavior

- Daytime: No lights triggered (enough sunlight)
- Nighttime: Motion triggers cool white lights at 70%
- Deactivation after 1 minute

Scenario 3: Morning Kitchen Boost

- 6:00 AM – 9:00 AM
- Motion detected triggers bright white light
- Scene auto-adjusts depending on weekday/weekend

Using platforms like **Home Assistant**, **SmartThings**, or **Alexa Routines**, you can combine these behaviors into "if-this-then-that" logic.

Tips for Successful Light Scene Automation

- **Label Scenes Clearly**: Give your scenes practical names like "Relax Evening" or "Workout Lights" for quick voice access.

- **Avoid Overautomation**: Don't automate every space. Focus on high-traffic or practical areas to keep things simple and effective.

- **Test and Adjust**: Light levels, motion sensitivity, and timer durations may need tweaking. Observe how your household interacts with the lights for a few days, then make adjustments.

- **Sync with Daylight**: Adjust your scene schedule throughout the year to account for seasonal light changes. Some hubs allow for sunrise/sunset-based automations.

Lighting is one of the most powerful tools in the smart home arsenal. Through thoughtfully crafted scenes and motion-activated automation, you can turn your home into a responsive, adaptive environment that enhances every part of your daily life. Whether it's the subtle glow guiding you down the stairs at midnight, or the energizing brightness in your morning routine, smart lighting creates comfort, efficiency, and atmosphere with minimal effort and investment.

Section 1: Cameras, Alarms, and Entry Sensors

In an age where digital convenience and home safety go hand in hand, smart security systems are no longer luxury items; they're becoming essential components of modern homes. Whether you're protecting a studio apartment or a suburban house, there are now countless affordable options for cameras, alarms, and entry sensors that can be easily installed without professional assistance or ongoing monthly fees. This section will guide you through the basics of budget-friendly security equipment, show you what to look for, and recommend solid, low-cost options that can help safeguard your home from unwanted intrusions.

Budget-Friendly Indoor and Outdoor Cameras

Security cameras are often the first thing people think of when considering smart home protection. They not only act as a deterrent to would-be intruders but also give you peace of mind through real-time monitoring and video playback. Fortunately, the market now offers a wide range of cameras at very reasonable prices, many of which include features that were previously exclusive to high-end systems.

Key Features to Look For

When choosing a camera, especially on a budget, focus on essential features that offer maximum value without unnecessary bells and whistles:

- **Video Resolution**: At a minimum, go for 1080p HD. This ensures clear images and better facial recognition in footage.
- **Night Vision**: Infrared or full-color night vision allows the camera to "see" in complete darkness.
- **Motion Detection**: Alerts you when movement is detected and can trigger recording or notifications.
- **Two-Way Audio**: Lets you hear what's happening and communicate with people near the camera.
- **Field of View**: A wider field of view (ideally 120° or more) covers more area with fewer cameras.
- **Cloud and/or Local Storage**: Choose a camera that supports SD cards for local storage or has free/low-cost cloud plans.
- **Weather Resistance**: Outdoor cameras should have an IP65 or higher rating to withstand rain, snow, and dust.
- **Smart Assistant Compatibility**: Cameras that work with Alexa, Google Assistant, or Apple HomeKit provide easier integration.

Recommended Budget Cameras

Here are a few reliable options that strike a good balance between affordability and function:

1. **Wyze Cam v3**

   - *Price*: Around $35
   - *Why It's Great*: Weather-resistant, color night vision, 1080p video, free 14-day cloud storage, and local microSD support.
   - *Best For*: Indoor and outdoor use.
   - *Platform Compatibility*: Works with Alexa and Google Assistant.
   - **Source**: https://www.wyze.com
   - **Confidence Level**: 95%

2. **Blink Outdoor 4**

   - *Price*: Around $60 per camera
   - *Why It's Great*: Long battery life (up to 2 years), wire-free installation, motion detection, and Alexa integration.
   - *Best For*: Outdoor home perimeters, sheds, garages.
   - *Platform Compatibility*: Alexa
   - **Source**: https://www.amazon.com/Blink-Outdoor
   - **Confidence Level**: 90%

3. **TP-Link Tapo C100**

   - *Price*: Around $25
   - *Why It's Great*: 1080p video, two-way audio, customizable motion zones, and local storage.
   - *Best For*: Indoor monitoring on a tight budget.
   - *Platform Compatibility*: Google Assistant, Alexa
   - **Source**: https://www.tp-link.com
   - **Confidence Level**: 90%

4. **Eufy Security Indoor Cam 2K**

   - *Price*: Around $40
   - *Why It's Great*: High-res 2K video, AI person detection, local storage with no subscription fees.
   - *Best For*: Nurseries, indoor hallways, and entryways.
   - *Platform Compatibility*: Works with Apple HomeKit, Google Assistant, Alexa
   - **Source**: https://www.eufylife.com
   - **Confidence Level**: 93%

DIY Alarm Systems and Entry Sensors

If you're on a mission to secure your home without locking yourself into a pricey monitoring contract, DIY alarm systems and sensors are the way to go. They offer self-monitoring, remote alerts, and integration with other smart devices; all while being user-friendly and wallet-conscious.

Components of a DIY Alarm System

A typical DIY home security kit includes:

- **Main Hub/Control Panel**: The brain of the system. Communicates with all connected devices.
- **Motion Sensors**: Detect movement in rooms or hallways.
- **Door/Window Sensors**: Trigger alerts when opened unexpectedly.
- **Siren**: Loud audible alarm to scare off intruders and alert you.
- **Key Fob/Keypad**: Arms and disarms the system without a smartphone.
- **Mobile App**: Enables remote control, alerts, and configuration.

Best DIY Systems (No Monthly Fees)

1. **Ring Alarm (Optional Subscription)**

   - *Price*: Starter kit around $200
   - *Why It's Great*: Easy setup, highly customizable, app-controlled. Subscription optional for monitoring.
   - *No-Contract Option*: You can self-monitor for free.
   - *Platform Compatibility*: Alexa
   - **Source**: https://ring.com
   - **Confidence Level**: 88%

2. **Abode Security Kit**

   - *Price*: Starts around $180
   - *Why It's Great*: Includes door/window sensors, motion sensors, and a base station. Self-monitoring available with automation.
   - *Platform Compatibility*: Alexa, Google Assistant, Apple HomeKit
   - **Source**: https://goabode.com
   - **Confidence Level**: 87%

3. **Kangaroo Home Security Kit**

   - *Price*: Around $100
   - *Why It's Great*: Very budget-friendly. Includes entry sensors, keypad, and optional cloud features.
   - *Best For*: Apartments or small homes.
   - **Source**: https://heykangaroo.com
   - **Confidence Level**: 85%

4. **SimpliSafe Essentials Kit**

- o *Price*: Starts at $250, often discounted
- o *Why It's Great*: Reliable, widely reviewed, cellular backup option, easy to scale.
- o *No-Contract Option*: Self-monitoring is free; paid professional monitoring optional.
- o **Source**: https://simplisafe.com
- o **Confidence Level**: 90%

Door and Window Sensors

These sensors are perhaps the most vital part of any home security system. They're simple to install and serve as your first line of defense.

Best Entry Sensors on a Budget

1. **YoLink Door Sensors**

   - o *Price*: Around $60 for a 4-pack
   - o *Why It's Great*: Long-range communication, low power consumption (battery lasts up to 5 years), compatible with Alexa and IFTTT.
   - o **Source**: https://www.yosmart.com
   - o **Confidence Level**: 92%

2. **GE Personal Security Door Alarm**

   - o *Price*: $12–$15
   - o *Why It's Great*: Extremely cheap and easy to use. No app, just a physical alarm that sounds when the door is opened.
   - o *Best For*: Non-tech-savvy users or temporary rentals.
   - o **Source**: https://www.gelighting.com
   - o **Confidence Level**: 85%

3. **Wyze Entry Sensor**

   - o *Price*: Around $30 for a 3-pack
   - o *Why It's Great*: Integrates with Wyze Cam, sends mobile alerts, and supports automation.
   - o **Source**: https://www.wyze.com
   - o **Confidence Level**: 90%

Easy Installation Tips

DIY smart security systems are designed for simplicity, but here are a few tips to make the setup even smoother:

- **Use Adhesive Tape or Mounting Brackets**: Most entry sensors and cameras come with peel-and-stick options or easy-screw mounts. Clean surfaces first to ensure a solid grip.
- **Download the App First**: Before you even open the box, install the system's companion app. Most of the setup process is guided through it.
- **Label Devices**: If you have multiple sensors, label them by room in the app for easy identification.
- **Test Before Final Mounting**: Check signal strength and sensor detection ranges by temporarily taping devices in place and testing functionality.
- **Check Internet/Wi-Fi Strength**: Weak Wi-Fi results in dropped footage and delays. Consider a mesh router or signal extender if needed.

You don't need to spend thousands of dollars or commit to long-term contracts to enjoy peace of mind in your home. Today's market offers powerful, budget-friendly indoor and outdoor cameras, as well as DIY alarm systems and sensors, that are reliable, easy to set up, and surprisingly effective.

By understanding what features matter most (high video resolution, smart motion alerts, and flexible storage) you can make informed decisions that protect your home and loved ones without draining your wallet. Combine smart cameras with entry sensors and a DIY alarm kit, and you'll have a highly effective security system at a fraction of the traditional cost.

Section 2: Remote Monitoring and Alerts

In the digital age, smart security systems have redefined what it means to protect your home. One of the most powerful features of these systems is their ability to provide remote monitoring and real-time alerts. This section explores how mobile notifications and video feeds keep you connected to your home from anywhere in the world, and how integrating smart assistants like Alexa, Google Assistant, or Siri enhances your home security through simple voice commands.

Mobile Notifications and Real-Time Video: How to Receive Alerts on Your Phone

One of the main reasons people invest in smart security systems is the peace of mind that comes from always being connected to what matters most; their home and family. Thanks to Wi-Fi-enabled cameras and sensors, your security system can alert you instantly if something unexpected occurs. Here's how it works and what you need to know to get the most from these features.

1. Understanding Mobile Notifications

Mobile notifications are real-time alerts that your smart home security system sends to your smartphone or tablet. These alerts can include:

- **Motion detection notifications**: Letting you know if someone (or something) is moving around your property.
- **Door and window sensor triggers**: Informing you if a door or window has been opened.
- **Camera activity alerts**: Notifying you when a person or vehicle is captured on camera.
- **Audio alerts**: If your security device picks up suspicious noises, like glass breaking or a smoke alarm sounding.
- **System status updates**: Informing you about battery levels, connectivity issues, or system arming/disarming.

To receive these notifications, all you need is:

- A **smartphone or tablet**
- An **internet connection**
- The official **app** for your security system (e.g., Arlo, Ring, Wyze, SimpliSafe, etc.)

Most of these apps allow you to **customize** your alert settings. You can choose what types of events trigger a notification and whether to receive push notifications, email alerts, or both. For instance, you might set your cameras to notify you only when motion is detected between 10 p.m. and 6 a.m., or you may want to ignore animal motion during the day.

2. Real-Time Video Streaming

Today's smart cameras go beyond passive recording. They allow you to **view live footage** directly from your smartphone, giving you an instant window into your home, backyard, or driveway. Whether you're at the office, on vacation, or just in another room, you can check in anytime.

Most smart cameras feature:

- **HD resolution**: Typically 1080p or higher, for clear images.
- **Infrared night vision**: So you can see even in complete darkness.
- **Two-way audio**: Letting you speak through the camera and listen to what's happening on the other end.
- **Cloud or local video storage**: So you can review footage later if needed.

These features are particularly useful for checking packages at your door, making sure your pets are safe, or verifying whether a motion alert is a real threat or a false alarm.

Pro tip: Some cameras, such as the Ring Video Doorbell or Arlo Pro 5S, offer **pre-roll video**, which records a few seconds before motion is detected, giving you a fuller picture of what happened.

3. Recommended Apps for Monitoring

- **Ring App**: Works with all Ring devices and allows two-way talk, real-time video, and instant motion alerts.
- **Arlo App**: Offers powerful features like animated previews of alerts and advanced AI motion detection.
- **Google Home App**: Works with Nest devices and provides seamless control across other Google-enabled products.
- **Smart Life App**: A universal app compatible with many budget-friendly third-party cameras and sensors.

Always ensure your phone's settings allow these apps to run in the background and push notifications in real time. Without the right permissions, you might miss an important alert.

Integrating with Smart Assistants: Using Voice Control to Check Home Security

Smart assistants are no longer novelties; they're central to how we interact with technology in the home. When integrated with your security system, assistants like Amazon Alexa, Google Assistant, or Apple Siri can enhance your ability to manage and monitor your setup using only your voice.

1. Benefits of Voice Control for Security

Integrating smart assistants provides:

- **Convenience**: No need to open an app; just say, "Alexa, show me the front door" or "Hey Google, is the back door locked?"
- **Speed**: In emergencies, voice commands may be faster than navigating an app.
- **Hands-Free Operation**: Perfect for busy moments; like when you're cooking or carrying groceries.

This hands-free control can be used for:

- Viewing live camera feeds on smart displays (like Echo Show, Google Nest Hub).
- Arming or disarming alarm systems (some require PIN codes).
- Checking the status of doors, locks, or motion sensors.
- Activating routines (e.g., "Goodnight" routine that locks doors, arms the alarm, and turns off lights).

2. Compatibility: What Works with What?

Most major smart security brands support smart assistant integration:

If you're an Apple user who relies heavily on Siri and HomeKit, make sure to choose devices explicitly labeled as HomeKit-compatible. These typically require an Apple Home Hub (like an Apple TV or HomePod).

3. Setting Up Voice Integration

The process will vary slightly depending on your smart assistant, but the general steps are:

For Alexa:

1. Open the Alexa app.
2. Tap on "Devices," then "Add Device."
3. Choose your device type (camera, sensor, etc.).
4. Link the appropriate skill (e.g., "Ring," "SimpliSafe").
5. Sign into your security account to authorize access.

For Google Assistant:

1. Open the Google Home app.
2. Tap "+" to add a device.
3. Select "Works with Google."
4. Search for your security device brand.
5. Link your account and authorize control.

For Siri/HomeKit:

1. Scan the HomeKit setup code (often found in your device's packaging).
2. Add the device to the Home app on your iPhone.
3. Organize devices into rooms and assign names for voice commands.

Once set up, you can create custom voice routines. For example, you might create a "Leaving Home" routine that says, "Alexa, I'm leaving," and triggers your system to lock doors, arm sensors, and lower the thermostat.

Real-Life Example: A Day in the Life with Remote Monitoring

Imagine this:

You're at work and your phone buzzes. The alert reads: "Motion detected at front door." You open the app and see a delivery person leaving a package. With two taps, you open the two-way audio and say, "Thank you! Please place it behind the planter." Moments later, you get another alert: "Front door sensor triggered." You open the camera feed again and see your teenager arriving home from school. That evening, as you're preparing for bed, you simply say, "Alexa, arm away mode," and the house is secured for the night.

This seamless flow from mobile alerts to smart assistant control is not just convenient; it's empowering. It gives you full control over your home's security, even when you're miles away.

Remote monitoring and alerts are at the heart of modern home security. Whether you want to see who's at your door, verify that your kids made it home safely, or ensure your house is locked up for the night, mobile notifications and smart assistant integration make it all possible. The best part? You can customize every part of the system to suit your lifestyle, preferences, and security concerns.

With a well-chosen combination of smart cameras, sensors, and voice assistant integrations, you can build a smart security system that keeps you connected, protected, and in control; wherever life takes you.

Section 1: Smart Thermostats and Fans

Controlling the temperature of your home efficiently not only keeps you comfortable but also has a significant impact on your energy consumption and utility bills. Smart thermostats and fans are at the core of modern climate control, offering users precise management of heating and cooling systems. With the ability to automate settings and access real-time data, these smart devices provide the tools necessary for optimizing both comfort and cost-effectiveness. In this section, we will explore the steps for installing a DIY smart thermostat and how to integrate smart plugs and IR blasters to control fans and air conditioners seamlessly.

Installing a DIY Smart Thermostat: Compatibility, Wiring Basics, and Setup

1. Why Choose a Smart Thermostat?

Smart thermostats allow users to create heating and cooling schedules, access and control their systems remotely, and learn from usage patterns to automatically adjust settings for optimal energy efficiency. Some advanced models can even use geofencing to know when you're away and adjust temperatures accordingly, helping reduce energy waste.

2. Compatibility Check

Before buying and installing a smart thermostat, it's essential to ensure compatibility with your existing HVAC system. Here's how:

- **Check your wiring**: Remove your current thermostat faceplate and look for wires labeled Rh, Rc, W, Y, G, C, etc. Most smart thermostats require a C-wire (common wire) for constant power.
- **Type of HVAC system**: Most residential homes use either a low-voltage (24V) system or high-voltage (line voltage) system. Smart thermostats typically work only with low-voltage systems.
- **Check brand-specific compatibility tools**: Websites like Nest, ecobee, and Honeywell offer compatibility checkers. Simply enter your current thermostat wire labels and get instant feedback.

3. Wiring Basics

Understanding the wiring of your thermostat can seem daunting, but it's manageable with the right guidance. The most common wire labels include:

- **R or Rh/Rc**: Power wire from the heating or cooling transformer
- **C**: Common wire (provides constant power)

- **W**: Controls the heating system
- **Y**: Controls the air conditioning system
- **G**: Controls the fan

If you lack a C-wire, don't worry; some thermostats include a power extender kit (PEK), or you can install an adapter or hire an electrician for rewiring.

4. Installation Steps

Once compatibility is confirmed, and you've reviewed the wiring basics, follow these steps:

1. **Turn off power** to your HVAC system at the breaker.
2. **Remove the old thermostat** and label each wire as you disconnect it.
3. **Mount the new thermostat's base plate** using the provided hardware.
4. **Connect wires** to the corresponding terminals on the new thermostat.
5. **Attach the thermostat display** and restore power.
6. **Follow the setup wizard** on the device or companion app.

Most installations take 30 to 60 minutes and require only basic tools: a screwdriver, wire labels, and sometimes a drill.

5. Recommended Smart Thermostats

- **Google Nest Learning Thermostat**: Learns your habits and programs itself. ($200+)
- **ecobee SmartThermostat**: Comes with a room sensor to manage hot or cold spots. ($250)
- **Wyze Smart Thermostat**: A budget-friendly option with core features. ($70)
- **Honeywell Home T9**: Flexible control with smart room sensors. ($200)

Controlling Fans and Air Conditioners: Using Smart Plugs or IR Blasters for Automation

Not every fan or air conditioner supports smart features out of the box, but that doesn't mean they can't be automated. By using smart plugs or IR (infrared) blasters, you can bring legacy appliances into your smart ecosystem.

1. Smart Plugs: Turn Devices On/Off Remotely

How they work: Smart plugs are simple adapters that plug into a standard outlet. You then plug your fan or air conditioner into the smart plug, allowing you to control power via an app or voice assistant.

What you can control:

- On/off power
- Scheduling
- Usage monitoring (on some models)

Limitations:

- Only effective if the appliance resumes its previous state when power is restored. Many newer A/C units and fans default to OFF when plugged back in.

Top smart plug recommendations:

- **TP-Link Kasa Smart Plug**: Easy app control, works with Alexa and Google.
- **Wyze Plug**: Affordable, supports scheduling and usage tracking.
- **Amazon Smart Plug**: Seamless integration with Alexa.

Use Case Example: You can set your smart plug to turn on a fan every weekday at 5:30 p.m., just before you return home, ensuring comfort without wasting energy all day.

2. IR Blasters: Remote Control for Traditional Devices

What they do: IR blasters act like universal remote controls that can send infrared signals to your A/C or fan, mimicking the original remote.

Setup basics:

1. Place the IR blaster in line of sight of the appliance.
2. Use the app to configure it with the correct brand and model.
3. Create automation routines or integrate with voice assistants.

Top IR blaster products:

- **BroadLink RM4 Mini**: Supports thousands of devices; works with Alexa and Google.
- **SwitchBot Hub Mini**: Easy setup; supports IFTTT and smart scenes.
- **Sofia Smart IR Blaster**: Good budget-friendly option with solid compatibility.

Advantages:

- More precise control than smart plugs.
- Can change temperature settings, fan speed, and modes.

Limitations:

- Requires clear line of sight.
- May not work with devices that use RF remotes instead of IR.

3. Combining Devices for Maximum Control

For ultimate control and efficiency, many users combine smart thermostats with smart plugs and IR blasters:

- Use a **smart thermostat** to control central HVAC.
- Use **IR blasters** to automate split-unit A/C systems.
- Use **smart plugs** for fans or portable heaters.

All these devices can be controlled via a single app or smart assistant, giving you unified climate control from anywhere.

4. Automating with Routines and Scenes

Most smart home platforms allow you to create routines or scenes:

- **"Good Morning"**: Turn on bedroom fan and adjust thermostat to a comfortable temperature.
- **"Away Mode"**: Turn off all fans and A/C units, lower thermostat to energy-saving setting.
- **"Cool Down House"**: Turn on IR-controlled A/C and set to 70°F at 4:30 p.m. daily.

These automations save time and reduce the need for manual adjustments, optimizing both convenience and energy usage.

Installing a DIY smart thermostat is an achievable project that can significantly enhance your home's energy efficiency. With proper planning, wiring knowledge, and the right tools, most homeowners can complete the job in under an hour. Meanwhile, even if you're not ready to upgrade your central HVAC system, smart plugs and IR blasters provide affordable, effective ways to control fans and air conditioners.

Together, these devices create a smart climate control system that keeps you comfortable year-round while reducing unnecessary energy consumption. Whether you're at home or away, you'll have the power to monitor, adjust, and optimize your environment with just a few taps or voice commands.

Section 2: Monitoring and Reducing Energy Use

Energy Monitoring Plugs and Apps

Tracking Your Consumption in Real-Time

One of the most accessible and budget-friendly methods for understanding how your home consumes energy is through the use of energy monitoring plugs and smart energy apps. These devices and applications are crucial components in a smart home setup for those who are determined to reduce their electricity bills and lower their environmental impact.

Energy monitoring plugs, also known as smart plugs with energy metering, are inserted between your electrical outlet and your appliance. Once installed, these plugs monitor the power draw of whatever is plugged into them. Brands such as TP-Link's Kasa Smart Plug HS110, Emporia Smart Plug, and Wyze Plug offer models that are both affordable and reliable.

Most of these smart plugs connect via Wi-Fi or Bluetooth and are controlled through a smartphone app. These apps provide a real-time dashboard that shows how much electricity a specific appliance is using at any given moment. For instance, if you plug your coffee maker into an energy monitoring plug, the app will display its wattage usage and let you know how much it costs to run it daily, weekly, or monthly.

More advanced systems like the Sense Energy Monitor or Emporia Vue connect to your home's electrical panel and provide a holistic view of your home's energy consumption. These systems can identify patterns in your energy use, such as peak times when your HVAC system is working the hardest, or which devices are using phantom energy when idle.

When you understand how each device contributes to your overall energy consumption, you're empowered to make informed decisions. You might discover that your old refrigerator is a power hog, or that your TV continues to draw significant power in standby mode. Identifying these inefficiencies is the first step toward reducing your energy usage and, by extension, your monthly utility bills.

Choosing the Right Tools

Choosing the right energy monitoring tools depends on your budget and how deep you want to go into your energy analysis. If you're just getting started, begin with two or three smart plugs on your most used appliances; typically your entertainment center, computer setup, and kitchen gadgets.

If you want a whole-home solution, consider investing in a system like the Sense or Emporia Vue, both of which require a bit more installation effort (usually inside your electrical panel) but deliver far more comprehensive data.

Regardless of the tool, always check compatibility with your smart hub (like Alexa, Google Home, or Home Assistant) to ensure seamless integration. Apps should allow for alerts, historical analysis, and preferably integration with IFTTT or automation routines.

Setting Schedules and Automation Rules

Automating Off-Peak Usage for Savings

Once you have real-time data about your energy consumption, the next step is automation. The goal is simple: reduce consumption during peak hours and take advantage of lower-cost energy periods. This practice is known as time-of-use optimization and can save you substantial money if your utility provider offers variable pricing.

Many smart plugs and appliances allow you to set schedules directly from their companion app. For example, if your utility provider charges less for electricity at night, you can schedule your dishwasher or washing machine to run during those hours. Similarly, you can automate your home office or entertainment system to power down completely at bedtime or during work hours.

Smart thermostats also contribute significantly to energy savings through scheduled heating and cooling cycles. For example, Google Nest and Ecobee models allow for intelligent learning or manual schedules where heating and cooling adjust based on when you're home or away. You can set the thermostat to lower the heat or air conditioning when you're sleeping or at work, and have it return to your desired comfort level just before you wake up or return home.

Smart lighting automation can also reduce power use. By creating scenes that use dimmed lighting during the evening or automate lights to turn off when a room is unoccupied, you avoid unnecessary power drain. Motion sensors and timers are inexpensive additions that enhance this effect.

Using Rules and Triggers to Maximize Efficiency

In addition to setting simple schedules, smart home systems allow for advanced automation through rules and triggers. These logic-based actions respond to specific conditions, which can significantly enhance efficiency and convenience.

For example, using a platform like Home Assistant or SmartThings, you could create a rule such as:

- *If no motion is detected in the living room for 15 minutes after 10 PM, then turn off all lights and entertainment systems.*
- *If energy usage exceeds 3000 watts at any time, send an alert or shut down non-essential devices.*
- *If the outside temperature drops below 50°F and someone is home, trigger the heater to turn on and circulate warm air.*

These rules take advantage of interconnected sensors, plugs, thermostats, and more to form a true smart ecosystem. Automation rules help prevent the human error of leaving devices on, and they tailor energy use to actual need, not just preset schedules.

You can also use smart routines provided by your digital assistants. Alexa's Routines, Google Home's Automations, and Home Assistant's Blueprints allow for highly customizable scenarios that react to a combination of time, location, device status, and more.

Practical Tips for Scheduling and Automation

1. **Start Simple**: Begin with time-based schedules for major appliances and work your way toward condition-based triggers.
2. **Use Templates**: Many apps and platforms offer pre-built automation templates that save setup time and ensure best practices.
3. **Regular Review**: Review your energy usage data monthly to adjust schedules and improve automation rules based on season, household changes, or utility pricing shifts.
4. **Test and Tweak**: It may take some time to fine-tune rules. Monitor results and adjust thresholds or trigger conditions to suit your actual lifestyle and energy goals.

Integration with Renewable Energy Sources

For households that have adopted solar power or other renewable energy sources, smart automation can align energy usage with times of peak generation. For example, if your solar panels generate the most electricity between 10 AM and 4 PM, automation rules can prioritize laundry, dishwashing, and charging of battery banks or electric vehicles during those hours.

Smart inverters and solar monitoring systems like Enphase and SolarEdge can integrate with smart home platforms, enabling even more granular control. Some systems allow you to see solar output in real time and shift loads accordingly, helping you get the most out of your investment.

Reducing Standby Power Use

Many electronics draw power even when turned off; a phenomenon known as phantom or vampire power. Smart plugs can completely shut off power to devices when not in use, eliminating this waste.

To take this further, consider grouping devices. For instance, plug your TV, sound system, and game console into a power strip connected to a smart plug. Schedule the plug to turn off overnight or during work hours. This small adjustment can reduce your bill and extend the lifespan of your electronics.

Data-Driven Efficiency

Monitoring and reducing energy use in your smart home doesn't have to be expensive or complicated. With a few smart plugs, a reliable app, and some well-thought-out schedules, you can begin to take real control of your consumption. As you become more comfortable with the tools and data, you can implement increasingly sophisticated automation routines that cut waste, reduce bills, and align perfectly with your lifestyle.

Energy efficiency isn't just a buzzword; it's a practical, money-saving strategy that benefits both your household and the planet. Through real-time monitoring and smart automation, your home becomes not just more intelligent, but also more responsible and cost-effective.

Chapter 6: Entertainment and Lifestyle Automation

Section 1: Media Centers and Smart Speakers

Setting Up Voice-Controlled Entertainment

In the modern smart home, entertainment is no longer limited to remote controls and manual toggles. By integrating voice-controlled entertainment systems, homeowners can enjoy a seamless media experience powered by smart assistants like Amazon Alexa, Google Assistant, or Apple's Siri. These systems provide effortless access to music, movies, TV shows, and streaming services through voice commands, bringing comfort and convenience to your daily life.

The Foundation of Voice-Controlled Entertainment

Setting up a voice-controlled media center begins with choosing a smart assistant that aligns with your preferences and ecosystem. Amazon Echo devices with Alexa are a popular choice due to wide compatibility and robust skill support. Google Nest devices work beautifully with Google services like YouTube and Chromecast. Apple's HomePod with Siri is ideal for users already invested in the Apple ecosystem.

Once your assistant is selected, you can link it to compatible media devices. These may include smart TVs (e.g., Samsung, LG, Sony), streaming devices (e.g., Fire TV, Chromecast, Roku), and speakers (e.g., Sonos, Bose). The setup usually involves installing the manufacturer's app, signing in to your streaming accounts, and connecting the assistant via its corresponding app (Alexa app, Google Home, or Apple Home).

Controlling TV, Music, and Streaming Services

With voice control activated, you can use simple commands like:

- "Alexa, play Stranger Things on Netflix."
- "Hey Google, play jazz music in the living room."
- "Hey Siri, turn on the TV and play Apple Music."

Many smart TVs come with built-in support for assistants or can be controlled using a compatible streaming device. If your TV isn't natively smart, devices like Amazon Fire Stick or Google Chromecast can bridge the gap. Voice commands can control power, volume, input sources, and media playback.

For music, linking Spotify, Apple Music, Amazon Music, or YouTube Music allows users to request specific songs, playlists, or genres. Multi-room audio can be configured by grouping multiple smart speakers together, creating a synchronized playback environment across your home.

Smart Speaker Integration Tips

To optimize performance:

- Place smart speakers near your primary entertainment devices.
- Ensure Wi-Fi coverage is strong in media rooms.
- Use specific device names when controlling (e.g., "Play on Living Room TV").
- Set up media defaults in your assistant's settings to avoid needing to specify the service every time.

Voice control doesn't just enhance convenience; it opens up accessibility. For elderly users or those with physical disabilities, being able to control entertainment through speech can be life-changing.

Creating Custom Voice Commands

Beyond simple playback commands, smart assistants offer the ability to create routines and custom voice shortcuts. These routines combine multiple actions into one command, personalizing the smart home experience.

Understanding Routines and Shortcuts

Routines are pre-programmed sequences of actions triggered by a single command. For instance, saying "Alexa, movie time" might:

- Dim the lights.
- Close the smart blinds.
- Turn on the TV.
- Launch your favorite streaming app.
- Adjust the thermostat.

Most smart assistant apps allow you to create these routines through an easy-to-use interface. In the Alexa app, go to Routines > Create Routine. In Google Home, use Automations. Apple users can set up Siri Shortcuts using the Shortcuts app.

Examples of Entertainment-Focused Routines

Here are a few sample routines you can customize:

1. **"Good Morning" Routine**:

     o Turn on lights gradually.
     o Play morning news or favorite podcast.
     o Display calendar and weather on smart display.
2. **"Workout Time" Routine**:

     o Start a workout playlist.
     o Turn on fan.

o   Adjust lighting to energizing brightness.
3. **"Game Night" Routine**:

   o   Turn on the TV.
   o   Launch a game console.
   o   Set color-changing smart bulbs to a vibrant theme.
4. **"Dinner Time" Routine**:

   o   Pause media playback.
   o   Dim or color-shift lights to warm tones.
   o   Play soft background music.

Creating Effective Custom Commands

To create commands that are easy to remember and use:

- Keep the trigger phrase short and intuitive.
- Avoid complex words or similar-sounding phrases.
- Use device names that reflect their location (e.g., "Living Room TV" instead of "Samsung Q60R").

You can also create alternate commands for the same routine. For instance, both "Let's relax" and "Movie mode" could trigger the same actions, allowing for more natural language use.

Using Third-Party Services and Apps

Third-party platforms like IFTTT (If This Then That) can enhance routines further. With IFTTT, you can:

- Trigger actions based on calendar events.
- Sync media control with external events (e.g., weather changes).
- Connect services not directly compatible with your assistant.

Automating with Presence Detection

Advanced routines can use presence detection (via phone GPS, Wi-Fi, or motion sensors) to automate media settings. For instance:

- When you enter the living room, your favorite radio station starts.
- When you leave the house, all media devices turn off.

This requires integration with smart home hubs like Home Assistant or SmartThings, which support conditional logic and device status tracking.

Using Smart Displays for Enhanced Control

Smart displays (e.g., Echo Show, Google Nest Hub) offer touch control and visual feedback. These are particularly useful in media rooms for:

- Browsing streaming content.
- Adjusting volume or skipping tracks.
- Viewing song lyrics or weather while music plays.

They also act as central hubs for managing all your smart devices, routines, and settings.

Voice-Controlled Gaming and VR

If you're into gaming, voice control can enhance immersion. PlayStation and Xbox support limited voice features through apps and integrations. With smart lighting, you can sync color changes with game intensity using tools like Philips Hue Sync.

In virtual reality setups, smart assistants can control the environment without removing your headset; changing lighting, music, or even activating a fan for added realism.

Budget Considerations

Voice-controlled entertainment can be built gradually. Start with a single smart speaker ($20–$50), then add a streaming device ($30–$60). Smart plugs ($10–$20) can automate older audio systems or TVs. Refurbished gear and bundle deals also offer cost-effective entry points.

Many devices work well even without expensive subscriptions. Free tiers of Spotify, YouTube, and Amazon services provide basic control. Avoid costly monthly fees by selecting media platforms with flexible access options.

Security and Privacy Concerns

Always consider privacy when adding voice assistants to your home:

- Review microphone permissions.
- Delete voice recordings regularly from your assistant's app.
- Use physical mute buttons when needed.
- Set PINs for purchases and restricted content.

Most platforms now offer transparency tools and voice history review options. Staying informed and configuring settings can mitigate potential privacy risks.

Voice-controlled media and entertainment aren't just a futuristic fantasy; they're accessible, practical, and budget-friendly tools that enrich everyday life. With just a few key devices and thoughtful customization, you can transform your media habits into a hands-free experience that fits your lifestyle. As technology continues to advance, integrating smart assistants, streaming platforms, and custom routines will only become more intuitive and rewarding.

Whether you're setting the mood for a romantic evening, powering through a workout, or enjoying family movie night, smart entertainment solutions offer unmatched control, comfort, and convenience; all within the sound of your voice.

Section 2: DIY Projects for Daily Convenience

Automating Coffee Makers, Curtains, and More

Home automation isn't limited to lighting or security; it extends to daily conveniences that can improve your comfort and save you time. With a bit of creativity and the right gadgets, you can automate everything from your morning coffee to the opening and closing of your curtains.

1. Automating Your Coffee Maker

One of the most popular and easy-to-automate appliances is the coffee maker. If your model is not already smart, don't worry; you can still integrate it into your smart home system affordably. Most basic drip coffee makers can be automated using a smart plug. By setting a schedule through your smart assistant or app, you can have your coffee ready when you wake up.

Choose a reliable smart plug compatible with your hub, like the TP-Link Kasa Smart Plug or the Amazon Smart Plug. Set it to power the coffee machine 10-15 minutes before you usually wake up. Just ensure the machine has water and coffee grounds loaded the night before. This simple automation can kick-start your day and become an essential part of your morning routine.

2. Automating Curtains and Blinds

Another small yet impactful automation project is motorizing your curtains or blinds. Several affordable kits are available that allow you to convert your traditional curtains into smart ones. For example, SwitchBot Curtain or Quoya Smart Curtain Systems offer DIY-friendly installations.

These devices can be scheduled to open in the morning with sunrise or close at sunset. You can also control them with voice commands through Alexa or Google Assistant. The benefit goes beyond comfort; automated curtains can help with energy efficiency by reducing heat gain in summer or retaining warmth in winter.

If you're on a tighter budget, consider using simple pulley systems combined with a stepper motor controlled by a Raspberry Pi or Arduino. These systems require some basic engineering but offer a fun challenge and a customized solution.

3. Automating Scent Diffusers and Air Purifiers

For a fresh and healthy indoor environment, automating scent diffusers or air purifiers can be both pleasant and beneficial. Smart plugs can again be your go-to solution. Set diffusers to turn on in the morning and evening for relaxation or use air quality sensors to activate purifiers when pollutant levels rise.

Devices like the Levoit Air Purifier with VeSync app control or the Meross Smart Diffuser can seamlessly integrate into your ecosystem. These small changes significantly boost your quality of life while remaining budget-conscious.

4. Automating Pet Feeders and Water Dispensers

If you have pets, smart feeders and dispensers can offer peace of mind and consistent care. Budget-friendly options like the PETLIBRO automatic feeder or the WOPET WiFi pet feeder allow you to schedule feedings and monitor food levels from your smartphone.

For an even more DIY approach, combine a servo motor with a food container and use a Raspberry Pi or ESP8266 microcontroller to control the dispensing times. This gives you full control over features and costs less than commercial models.

Subsection 2: Making Your Own Smart Mirror or Display

Smart mirrors and displays add a futuristic flair to your home and provide useful information at a glance, such as weather updates, calendar events, and news headlines. With the rise of single-board computers like the Raspberry Pi, these devices are no longer restricted to tech experts.

1. DIY Smart Mirror: The Basics

A smart mirror is essentially a two-way mirror placed over a monitor that displays digital content via a connected Raspberry Pi. Building one requires a few essential materials:

- A Raspberry Pi 3 or 4
- A monitor (repurposed or inexpensive screen)
- A two-way acrylic mirror
- A wooden or plastic frame
- Power supply and HDMI cable

Once assembled, install MagicMirror²; an open-source platform with modular components that let you customize the display. You can show time, date, weather, Google Calendar, traffic updates, news feeds, and more.

You can extend its functionality using voice control, motion sensors to turn it on/off, or even facial recognition. While costs may vary depending on your monitor choice, a basic smart mirror can be built for under $150.

2. Smart Display: Raspberry Pi Dashboard

If you prefer a dashboard-style display instead of a mirror, a Raspberry Pi touchscreen setup is ideal. These compact systems are great for placing in the kitchen or living room. You can configure dashboards with software like Dakboard, Home Assistant dashboards, or custom-built web UIs.

For instance, a wall-mounted dashboard can show:

- Your smart home control panel (lights, locks, sensors)
- Family schedules and shared to-do lists
- Weather and air quality updates
- Media and music controls

A 7- to 10-inch touchscreen can be purchased affordably, and the entire setup can be accomplished for less than $120. These displays serve as control centers for your home automation system, enhancing usability and access.

3. Add-Ons and Upgrades

Once you've built a basic smart mirror or display, you can enhance it further:

- Add voice control using a USB microphone and Mycroft AI or Google Assistant SDK.
- Use sensors to detect presence and turn on the screen automatically.
- Integrate your calendar, emails, or smart camera feeds.

These upgrades transform your DIY gadget into a dynamic, interactive tool that seamlessly integrates with the rest of your smart home.

4. Educational and Fun

DIY projects like these aren't just functional; they're also excellent learning tools. Whether you're exploring Linux for the first time, learning Python, or diving into IoT systems, building a smart mirror or dashboard boosts your technical skills. If you have children, involving them in these projects can be a great educational activity.

Entertainment and lifestyle automation goes beyond just comfort; it personalizes your space to suit your daily rhythms. Whether it's having coffee ready when you wake, controlling your curtains with a command, or viewing your schedule on a futuristic smart mirror, each project adds value and sophistication to your home.

With budget-conscious tools like smart plugs and Raspberry Pi, there's no need to spend thousands on automation. Creativity, a bit of DIY enthusiasm, and some basic equipment are all you need to create a smart home that fits your life.

Are you ready to dive into more advanced DIY automation? In the next chapter, we'll explore how to take your skills further with advanced integrations and personalized routines.

Section 1: Keeping Your Smart Home Secure

As smart homes become more popular, so do the risks associated with connected technology. While the benefits of automation and convenience are significant, they come with responsibilities; particularly when it comes to security. A well-maintained smart home isn't just about ensuring everything runs smoothly; it's about making sure your data, privacy, and devices are protected from digital intrusions and operational failures.

Protecting Your Devices from Hacking

The thought of a stranger taking control of your security cameras or speaking through your smart speaker is unsettling, but unfortunately, it's not impossible. Cybercriminals often look for unsecured smart devices as easy targets. Luckily, there are straightforward steps you can take to secure your home network and connected gadgets.

1.1 Strengthen Your Wi-Fi Network

Your Wi-Fi is the main gateway to all smart devices, so securing it is crucial.

- **Change Default Settings:** Many routers and smart devices come with default usernames and passwords, which are widely known and searchable. Change them immediately.
- **Use WPA3 or WPA2 Encryption:** Ensure your Wi-Fi network uses strong encryption like WPA2 or WPA3. This prevents unauthorized access.
- **Create a Separate Guest Network:** Smart devices don't need access to your computers or smartphones. Segment them on a separate guest network to limit exposure.

1.2 Use Strong, Unique Passwords

One of the most basic yet overlooked security measures is using strong passwords.

- **Avoid Reusing Passwords:** Each device or service should have its own password. Use a password manager if needed.
- **Enable Two-Factor Authentication (2FA):** Where available, enable 2FA to add an extra layer of protection.
- **Beware of Phishing Attacks:** Avoid clicking on links in suspicious emails or texts, especially those requesting password changes or account verification.

1.3 Choose Trusted Brands and Update Firmware

The smart home market is flooded with cheap devices that may not be built with security in mind.

- **Buy Reputable Brands:** Stick to manufacturers that are known for regularly updating their products.

- **Update Firmware Regularly:** Manufacturers release updates to patch vulnerabilities. Make it a habit to check for firmware updates monthly.
- **Avoid Unsupported Devices:** If a product is no longer supported with updates, it may become a security liability.

1.4 Secure Voice Assistants

Voice assistants like Alexa, Google Assistant, or Siri are incredibly useful—but they're also always listening.

- **Review Permissions:** Go into your assistant's app and review what it has access to.
- **Turn Off Mic When Not Needed:** Many smart speakers have a physical button to mute the microphone. Use it when privacy is important.
- **Delete Voice History:** Periodically delete your voice history from the assistant's app or website to enhance privacy.

Regular Updates and Backups

Keeping your smart home functional and secure over time means staying proactive. That involves more than just plugging things in and forgetting about them. Regular maintenance, including software updates and backups, can prevent a multitude of issues.

2.1 Importance of Regular Updates

Software updates are not just about adding new features; they often patch security vulnerabilities that have been discovered since the last update.

- **Schedule Time for Updates:** Set a monthly reminder to check all devices for firmware and app updates.
- **Enable Auto-Updates Where Possible:** Some apps and platforms allow automatic updates. Enable this option when available.
- **Stay Informed:** Follow the brands of your smart devices on social media or join online forums to stay informed about critical updates.

2.2 Back Up Your Settings and Data

If a device fails or needs to be reset, having a backup can save you time and frustration.

- **Use Cloud Services:** Many smart home platforms like Google Home and Alexa save settings to the cloud automatically.
- **Export Configurations:** Platforms like Home Assistant allow you to export your entire configuration. Do this regularly, especially after major changes.
- **Back Up Locally:** If you're running a local server (like Raspberry Pi with Home Assistant), back it up to a USB drive or external hard disk.

2.3 Monitor Device Performance

Regularly checking the performance of your devices can help you catch problems early.

- **Check for Slow Response Times:** A delay could be a sign of network issues or device failure.
- **Inspect Devices Physically:** Make sure nothing is overheating or showing signs of wear.
- **Replace Batteries Promptly:** Many devices like motion sensors and door alarms run on batteries. Keep extras handy and set a schedule to check power levels.

2.4 Perform Routine Audits

Taking inventory of your system every few months can help you keep things running smoothly.

- **Update Device List:** Keep a log of all your smart devices, their locations, and software versions.
- **Review Automations:** Sometimes rules you set up months ago are no longer relevant or efficient. Clean them up periodically.
- **Test Security Features:** Trigger your alarms or test your cameras to ensure everything works as expected.

Conclusion: Build Security into Your Routine

Smart home technology brings unmatched convenience, but it also creates new responsibilities. The best way to enjoy your automated home is to be mindful of its vulnerabilities and actively maintain its digital and physical health. Just as you would lock your doors and check the smoke detectors in a traditional home, your smart home needs regular care to remain a safe, reliable sanctuary.

With the right approach to cybersecurity and maintenance, your smart home can thrive; without draining your budget or causing stress. As we move into the next section, we'll explore how to expand your smart home without starting from scratch, keeping your investment scalable and future-proof.

Section 2: Planning for Growth

Scaling Your System Affordably

One of the great advantages of building your own smart home is the flexibility to start small and expand gradually. Unlike traditional home upgrades that require massive up-front costs and complex installations, smart home systems can grow room by room, device by device, and still stay budget-friendly. Planning for affordable growth starts with making smart choices early on and maintaining a clear vision of your future needs.

Start with a Scalable Hub

When beginning your smart home journey, choose a platform that supports a wide range of devices and has good long-term support. Hubs like Amazon Alexa, Google Home, and Home Assistant all offer expandable ecosystems. For instance, if you begin with Alexa-compatible smart plugs and bulbs, you can later add thermostats, security devices, or even smart appliances without changing your base system. Ensuring your hub supports popular protocols like Zigbee or Z-Wave also increases your options.

Use Modular Devices

Many smart devices today are modular, meaning you can add them one at a time without breaking the bank. Start with basics (perhaps just a few smart bulbs or a single security camera) and expand as your budget allows. For lighting, choose systems that support mesh networking, so adding a new bulb strengthens the network instead of stressing it. For security, you might install a video doorbell first and later add indoor motion sensors or smart locks.

Upgrade by Priority

Set clear goals about which areas of your home will benefit most from smart features. Common starter rooms include living rooms (for entertainment automation), kitchens (for convenience), and entryways (for security). Once these areas are automated, consider adding devices to bedrooms, bathrooms, or outdoor spaces. Rank your needs by potential impact: for instance, energy savings from automating your HVAC might take priority over smart window shades.

Budgeting for Additions

Stick to a monthly or quarterly smart home budget. Allocate funds for one new device or upgrade at a time. Look for sales events (Black Friday, Prime Day, or local tech deals) to buy devices at reduced prices. Refurbished or open-box items can also provide significant savings without compromising quality. Set up price alerts for specific gadgets and wait for deals to make your purchases.

Document and Label Everything

As your system grows, keeping track of devices becomes more complex. Maintain a digital inventory of all your smart gadgets, including their location, model numbers, MAC addresses, firmware version, and connected platforms. Label power adapters and cables with names or color codes. This small step can save hours when troubleshooting or upgrading your system in the future.

Keep Power and Network in Mind

With more devices comes increased strain on your home's Wi-Fi and power infrastructure. Plan for additional surge protectors, power strips, and perhaps even a dedicated breaker if your automation needs expand significantly. Mesh Wi-Fi systems or strategically placed range extenders ensure stable connections throughout your home.

Stay Open to Interoperability

Look for devices that are compatible with multiple platforms. The Matter protocol, an industry-wide standard developed by Apple, Google, Amazon, and others, aims to unify smart home devices and simplify compatibility. By choosing Matter-supported gadgets, you're future-proofing your system and making it easier to switch hubs if needed.

Building a Community or Sharing Your Projects

Your smart home journey doesn't have to be a solo adventure. In fact, some of the best learning and inspiration comes from the broader DIY smart home community. By connecting with others (online or in person) you can trade ideas, solve problems faster, and even discover innovative solutions you hadn't considered. Sharing your progress helps others while keeping you motivated and engaged.

Join Online Forums and Groups

Sites like Reddit (r/homeautomation), SmartThings Community, Home Assistant forums, and DIY subreddits are teeming with passionate tinkerers who love sharing tips, troubleshooting problems, and recommending devices. Whether you're troubleshooting a finicky motion sensor or debating between smart blinds, chances are someone has already tackled the issue. Ask questions, share your successes, and provide feedback to others.

Watch and Contribute to YouTube Channels

YouTube is a goldmine of DIY smart home content. Many creators walk you through installations, reviews, and hacks in detail. Some even test compatibility between devices to help others make better decisions. Once you gain confidence, consider uploading your own walkthroughs or time-lapse videos. Even simple recordings can help others get started and learn from your experience.

Start a Blog or Social Media Page

If you enjoy writing or photography, consider documenting your smart home projects in a blog. Share the step-by-step process, product reviews, cost breakdowns, and lessons learned. Platforms like Medium, WordPress, or even a dedicated Instagram page can turn your personal progress into a valuable community resource. Over time, your posts may become reference material for beginners.

Attend or Host Local Meetups

Tech stores, maker spaces, and public libraries sometimes host smart home events or workshops. Attending these meetups allows you to see products in action and exchange ideas with local DIYers. You can even start a small meetup group in your neighborhood to showcase your projects and discuss ideas face-to-face.

Stay Inspired by Project Showcases

Follow hashtags like #smarthome, #diyautomation, or #homeassistant on social media platforms to keep up with the latest trends and ideas. Seeing what others accomplish on a shoestring budget can inspire your next project. Maybe someone built an automated chicken coop or a Bluetooth plant watering system; seeing their creativity might unlock new ideas for your own home.

Be Transparent About Mistakes

Every smart home enthusiast makes mistakes. Maybe you installed a switch upside-down, bought a device that wouldn't integrate, or misjudged Wi-Fi coverage. Sharing your failures is just as helpful as showcasing your wins. Documenting what didn't work can be a huge service to others, and it builds credibility and authenticity in the DIY community.

Use GitHub and Open Source Projects

If you're tech-savvy or interested in coding, GitHub is home to many open-source smart home projects. From custom scripts for Home Assistant to DIY smart mirrors and energy dashboards, these tools can significantly expand your home's capabilities. You can fork existing projects or contribute your own ideas to help improve the tools the community uses.

Stay Updated and Keep Learning

Technology evolves quickly. Devices gain new features, apps improve, and standards change. Keep learning through newsletters, YouTube subscriptions, or RSS feeds from your favorite blogs. Knowing what's around the corner (like Matter updates, improved AI assistants, or lower-cost gadgets) can help you plan smart purchases and avoid obsolescence.

Teach Others and Encourage Curiosity

If someone in your family or friend circle is interested in automation, show them how your system works. Offer to help them install their first smart bulb or configure their Wi-Fi for better coverage. Teaching others not only reinforces your own knowledge, it cultivates a sense of community and shared growth.

Building a DIY smart home on a budget is an ongoing process; one where growth is both practical and rewarding. By making informed, incremental upgrades and connecting with a wider community of DIYers, you not only expand your home's functionality, but also your own knowledge and creativity. Start small, stay curious, and remember: each new project is a step toward a smarter, more efficient, and more enjoyable living space.

Conclusion: Empowering Your Home, Your Way

As we reach the final chapter of *DIY Smart Home on a Budget*, one truth should stand out: smart living is not reserved for the wealthy or the highly technical; it's accessible to anyone with curiosity, a modest budget, and a willingness to learn.

Throughout this book, you've explored the complete journey of building your own smart home system from the ground up. You've discovered how to plan, purchase, and install everything from lighting and climate controls to security systems and media hubs; all while keeping your spending in check. With every chapter, you've gained not just practical skills, but a deeper understanding of how connected technology can simplify daily life, improve efficiency, and create a more personalized living environment.

The benefits of DIY smart homes are clear: lower energy bills, improved comfort, enhanced security, and the ability to control your environment with a simple command or automated routine. But beyond convenience, this process teaches problem-solving, creativity, and digital literacy; valuable skills in today's tech-driven world.

Remember, smart home technology is a journey, not a destination. Start small, grow at your own pace, and don't be afraid to experiment. Mistakes are part of the learning process, and every device you install brings you closer to a home that responds to your needs.

Stay curious. Keep building. And most of all, share your knowledge. Whether it's helping a friend automate their coffee maker or posting your setup online, your experience can inspire others to take control of their space too.

Your home is now smarter, more efficient, and uniquely yours. Welcome to the future; one you built yourself.

www.ingramcontent.com/pod-product-compliance
Lightning Source LLC
Chambersburg PA
CBHW071032050326

40689CB00014B/3622